Pebble® Plus

Countries

Kenya

by Christine Juarez

Consulting Editor: Gail Saunders-Smith, PhD

CAPSTONE PRESS
a capstone imprint

Pebble Plus is published by Capstone Press,
1710 Roe Crest Drive, North Mankato, Minnesota 56003
www.capstonepub.com

Library of Congress Cataloging-in-Publication Data
Juarez, Christine, 1976–
  Kenya / by Christine Juarez.
    pages cm.—(Pebble plus. Countries.)
  Includes bibliographical references and index.
  Summary: "Simple text and full-color photographs illustrate the land, animals, and people of Kenya"—Provided by publisher.
  ISBN 978-1-4765-4229-4 (library binding)—ISBN 978-1-4765-6044-1 (ebook PDF)
1. Kenya—Juvenile literature. I. Title.
  DT433.522J83 2014
  967.62—dc23   2013031562

Editorial Credits
Erika L. Shores, editor; Bobbie Nuytten, designer; Tracy Cummins, media researcher; Laura Manthe, production specialist

Photo Credits
Flickr: Mark Skipper, 13; Getty Images: Nigel Pavitt, 11; Newscom: DANIEL IRUNGU/EPA, 15, Sergio Pitamitz/Robert Harding, 19, Stephen Morrison/EPA, 17; Photos.com: Stockbyte, 22; Shutterstock: Andrzej Kubik, 1, Itinerant Lens, 9, Ivsanmas, 4, KA Photography KEVM111, 21, Natalia Pushchina, 5, Ohmega1982, back cover (globe), Oleg_Mit, 22, Paul Banton, cover, PHOTOCREO/Michal Bednarek, 7, sahua d, cover, 1 (design element)

Note to Parents and Teachers

The Countries set supports national social studies standards related to people, places, and culture. This book describes and illustrates Kenya. The images support early readers in understanding the text. The repetition of words and phrases helps early readers learn new words. This book also introduces early readers to subject-specific vocabulary words, which are defined in the Glossary section. Early readers may need assistance to read some words and to use the Table of Contents, Glossary, Read More, Internet Sites, and Index sections of the book.

Printed in the United States of America in North Mankato, Minnesota.
092013   007775CGS14

Table of Contents

Where Is Kenya? 4

Landforms 6

Animals 8

Language and Population 10

Food 12

Celebrations 14

Where People Work 16

Transportation 18

Famous Sight 20

Country Facts 22

Critical Thinking Using the
Common Core 22

Glossary 23

Read More 24

Internet Sites 24

Index 24

Where Is Kenya?

Kenya is a country in eastern Africa. It is about the size of the U.S. state of Texas. Kenya's capital is Nairobi.

KENYA

★*Nairobi*

Landforms

Kenya has many landforms.
Beaches line the coast of the
Indian Ocean. Savannas and
the Chalbi Desert are north of the
coasts. Mountains are in the west.

Animals

In Kenya, lions and cheetahs chase antelope across savannas. Hippos cool themselves in muddy rivers. Elephants, zebras, and giraffes also roam Kenya.

Language and Population

Kenya has 44 million people.

Most Kenyans live in the countryside.

Kenyans speak Kiswahili or English.

Other languages are spoken by
different groups of native people.

11

Food

Corn is the main food in Kenya.
Ugali is a common dish. It is
made of corn flour and water.
It becomes a dough that Kenyans
eat alongside vegetables or meat.

13

Celebrations

Kenyans celebrate Jamhuri Day
on December 12. It marks the day
Kenya became its own country.
People enjoy large meals,
dancing, and parades.

Where People Work

Most Kenyans are farmers. Coffee beans and tea grow on large farms. Farmers sell these crops for money. On smaller farms, people grow corn to feed their families.

Transportation

Most Kenyans walk from place to place. In cities, people might take buses or taxis. People ride trains between large cities.

Famous Sight

People from all over the world come to see Kenya's wildlife. Visitors to Nairobi National Park look for lions, cheetahs, rhinos, giraffes, and zebras.

21

Country Facts

Name: Republic of Kenya

Capital: Nairobi

Population: 44,037,656 (July 2013 estimate)

Size: 224,962 square miles (582,649 square kilometers)

Languages: English, Kiswahili, and many native languages

Main Crops: tea, coffee, corn, wheat, sugarcane, fruit

Kenya's flag

Money: Kenyan shilling

Critical Thinking Using the Common Core

1. Many Kenyan meals include corn. Name some ways in which corn is used. (Key Ideas and Details)

2. All kinds of wildlife live in Nairobi National Park. What might be some of the reasons they live there and not in the wild? (Integration of Knowledge and Ideas)

Glossary

antelope—an animal that looks like a large deer and runs very fast

capital—the city in a country where the government is based

celebrate—to do something fun on a special day

coast—land near an ocean or sea

crop—a plant farmers grow in large amounts; usually for food

desert—a dry area with little rain

landform—a natural feature of the land

language—the way people speak or talk

national park—land set aside by a country in order to keep the plant and animal life safe

native—having to do with people who were born in a certain place

savanna—a flat, grassy area of land with few or no trees

taxi—a car with a driver whom you pay to take you where you want to go

Read More

Kras, Sarah Louise. *Kenya in Colors*. World of Colors. Mankato, Minn.: Capstone Press, 2009.

Tuchman, Gail. *Safari*. Washington, D.C.: National Geographic, 2010.

Ward, Chris. *Discover Kenya*. Discover Countries. New York: PowerKids Press, 2010.

Internet Sites

FactHound offers a safe, fun way to find Internet sites related to this book. All of the sites on FactHound have been researched by our staff.

Here's all you do:
Visit *www.facthound.com*
Type in this code: 9781476542294

Super-cool stuff!

Check out projects, games and lots more at
www.capstonekids.com

Index

animals, 8, 20

capital, 4, 22

crops, 16, 22

farming, 16

flag, 22

food, 12, 14, 16

Jamhuri Day, 14

landforms, 6

languages, 10, 22

money, 16, 22

Nairobi National
   Park, 20

population, 10, 22

savannas, 6, 8

size, 4, 22

transportation, 18

Word Count: 224   Grade: 1   Early-Intervention Level: 20